PRINCIPLES
OF
WINNING

HOW TO USE THE TIME TESTED PRINCIPLES
OF BUILDING SUCCESS AND
WEALTH OVER TIME

MARK MCGUNEGILL

PRIMIX
PUBLISHING
THE WRITE CHOICE

Primix Publishing
11620 Wilshire Blvd
Suite 900, West Wilshire Center, Los Angeles, CA, 90025
www.primixpublishing.com
Phone: 1-800-538-5788

Published by Primix Publishing: 04/23/2024

ISBN: 979-8-89194-133-5(sc)
ISBN: 979-8-89194-134-2(e)

Library of Congress Control Number: 2024904959

CONTENTS

CHAPTER 1

SELF-CONTROL

"Like a city whose walls are broken down is a man who lacks self-control."

Proverbs 25:28

There is a reason why I decided to place this chapter on self-control first in this book. That is because it is the most difficult and the most important principle to master. You must work on this principle daily starting today, and strengthen it until it becomes a solid foundation on which to build your success. Understand, that even if you learn and practice all of the other amazing principles that you will read about in this book, the house of success that you build will ultimately come crashing down if you do not exercise the virtue of self-control.

First, let us define what self-control is versus its close cousin, discipline, which we will discuss more thoroughly in a later chapter. Self-control is the ability to stop yourself from taking harmful or negative action, when you would otherwise desire to do so. Lack of self-control comes upon us when we face temptation to act against our own values and interests. It also includes, harming others by acting impulsively without thinking or caring, which ultimately comes back to harm us as well. Giving in to negative emotions such as hatred, greed, lust, and arrogance, can deplete your self-control strength. But if you can identify the lapse in judgement, you will then learn to identify the negative emotions within you, making it easier to avoid such situations in the future. This is why you must learn to recognize these feelings when they arise within you, and deploy your reasoning mind to overpower them. It can be difficult to do, but the muscle of self-control can grow stronger with use. The beginning of it all starts with making the right decisions. Consistent good decisions turn bad habits into good habits, and once something has become a habit, it is far easier to maintain. It is important to develop good habits in time management, work, health, saving, investing, etc. Making good decisions and taking right actions gets into the principle of developing discipline. As we will develop in the next chapter, discipline is the ability to take positive action that will advance yourself or your goals even when you don't feel like doing it. Discipline is needed to help you to build what you want. But self-control is needed to help you preserve what you have built, and everything else that you have. It does you no good to build a beautiful house, only to put a torch to it and burn it all down. Self-control must be the foundation of everything else you do. It is the insurance policy against losing what you have gained, to guarantee that you will ultimately move forward, and not backward.

When it comes right down to it, winning, or financial success is nothing more than the positive application of simple mathematics on a consistent basis. This is why a high school dropout can rise to become a multi-millionaire by finding ways to make small profits, and then repeating the process many many times. But it also requires that person to not sabotage himself or herself along the way by wasteful spending, distractions, or harmful addictions. Since we are all humans and have inherent weaknesses, there is often a disconnect between knowing what is harmful, and avoiding it, and knowing what is beneficial, and doing it. We often rationalize in our minds, that the short-term satisfaction of giving into a harmful temptation can be justified by taking out a small withdrawal from our future success account. We may reason to ourselves that those future benefits are a long way off, but the pleasure we see is immediate. Taking positive action consistently, without constantly getting off course due to lack of self-control, will definitely move you closer to your most valuable purpose.

Many would suggest that success is mostly a matter of luck. But just look at the numerous cases of lottery winners, or big jackpot winners at the casino, or those who inherit large family fortunes. There are many true accounts of people who have suddenly come into possession of a large amount of money, which they did not work for, or do anything to earn. For the people who never really understood the value of money, or how to make it grow, many faced the nightmare of losing it all, and much more. Even worse, are those who never realize a big windfall or major financial success. But they spend their limited resources and time trying to achieve a quick and easy big win. Without exercising rational thought or self-control, people like this will fall prey to get-rich-quick scams, con artists, and gambling addiction. They often do not understand that financial success does not rely on luck, but on mathematics. Everyone has their share of good luck and bad luck, of success and failure. Let's take a look at casino gambling for a moment. Casinos would never stay in business if everyone who placed a bet always lost and never won anything. Nobody would ever go back, and word would get around until people just stayed away. Soon, they would have no customers and no revenue. But casinos attract customers back by paying out many small wins, the occasional intermediate size win, and the rare major win. This gives people the dopamine rush that urges them on to keep playing, thinking that the next, bigger win will come anytime.

If someone visits a casino with any frequency, they will win and lose over and over and be up and down. The casino has the long-term mathematical edge on every game, and they know that they have a psychological edge on most players. The average player will gamble only for the fun and excitement. Because of this, even if they are winning and up at the moment, they will usually not stop, but continue to play until they lose all that they have won and more. There are however, a very small percentage of people who win and keep more than they lose over time, and beat the odds. These people often make a supplemental income by playing games of skill or chance. But what separates the professional gambler from the vast majority of the population is primarily, the attitude and intention of their purpose. Their purpose is purely mathematical. They make profits by fully understanding the math, the probabilities, and the best strategies of the games they are playing. Advantage players and professional gamblers approach it like a business. They see it as their job, and one that demands total attention, and focus. So for them, there is no room for drinking, socializing, or having fun. As a result, the professional gambler has developed his self-control and discipline levels through the stratosphere. Even though he also has losing sessions, he knows that with knowledge, skill, discipline, and self-control, he can have long-term success. This example is not meant to advocate gambling as a profession. But it is only to illustrate the incredible overcoming power one has who has mastered self-control.

The average person with little or no self-control approaches most activities or goals (if they have goals) emotionally. This means that they do it because of the way it makes them feel. You can see how this can easily lead to harmful additions of all kinds. The person with healthy levels of self-control sees that every activity has a rational purpose, even if it is having fun. Self-control allows us to use our reasoning mind, rather than our emotions to justify, validate, and if necessary, limit all of our activities to require that they conform to our values, goals, and purpose.

Self-control is the mental wall that we must build around our feelings and passions, so that they are contained until we decide when, and to what degree, to release them. Everyone who wants to be successful must set specific goals that give him a path and a direction to follow. Goals should be short-term, intermediate, and long-term. They should stretch your limits and sometimes move you out of complacency. But remember this very important fact about setting goals. A valid goal can only be something over which you have complete control. Namely, you only set goals that describe actions that you alone will take. Your goals cannot depend on the actions of others.

This is not to say that you cannot influence the actions of others, but their response or lack of it cannot be a valid goal for you. For example: If you were a sales person who made a commission on every product you sold, an invalid goal for you would be to say, "I'm going to sell five units this week." But, in order to sell, it takes another human being who must make the decision to buy. Instead, a more valid goal would be to say, "I'm going to make 20 sales presentations this week." The difference is that you can control what you do, but you do not ultimately control what others do. When you start accomplishing realistic goals, one after the other, you will start to see how discipline and self-control really pay off in your life.

It is self-control that your mind uses to sift out good from bad, effective from ineffective. You must be about your higher purpose always. Remember that you are not in competition with others, but with yourself. You cannot be the best at anything. There will always be someone better. But you can always be better than you were yesterday, or last month, or last year. In so doing, you become a different person, and a better person.

CHAPTER 2

DISCIPLINE

"Discipline is the bridge between goals and accomplishments."
Jim Rohn

Discipline can be defined as the ability to move you closer to a goal or purpose, even when you otherwise would not want to. There are really two kinds of discipline. We are all familiar with the discipline that is imposed on us by others, such as from family, school, the military, or an employer. This is the discipline which is set by others and carries almost immediate consequences for non-compliance. The other type of discipline, which is far more important to your success, is self-discipline. This is when we challenge ourselves daily to do whatever it takes to improve ourselves or reach our goals. With self-discipline, there is nobody else to impose penalties on us for not doing the things that we ought to do. This is why self-discipline is only found in highly successful people. When you apply it, there is no immediate positive or negative reinforcement. It must first start with a decision to act, followed by an absolute commitment to follow through until the objective is reached. You must have faith in the reward to come.

Because of the intense, inner commitment required, it is best to work on only a few disciplines at a time at first. Decide which are the most important actions that must be taken to move your goals forward. Do not try to squeeze them all too close together within the same time frame. You might be setting yourself up for failure.

Discipline is the characteristic most often associated with achieving goals. So it is within your power to set goals and to make them achievable. When you understand the control that you have in reaching one objective after another, a true feeling of power and confidence will fill you with excitement, knowing that it is only a matter of time before you reach any realistic goal. It is like inventing a game in which you set the objective, you make the rules, and you always have the advantage. However, before you begin to set goals and move toward them, first realize that they must be valid goals. A valid goal must meet the following three requirements: **1.** It must be possible. The goal cannot violate the physical laws of nature, nor can it be beyond anything you can physically accomplish yourself. **2.** The goal cannot be immoral. You should never set a goal that would result in harm to others, or violate the laws of God and man. **3.** Your goal cannot depend on the actions of others. A valid goal must be completely under your control to accomplish, otherwise, it is not a goal, it is only a wish. Outside of these very specific but broad limitations, there remains a world of possibilities for you to conquer. Of course, not everything in life is a direct result of our own actions. King Solomon said it best.

"The race is not to the swift or the battle to the strong, nor does food come to the wise or wealth to the brilliant or favor to the learned: But time and chance happen to them all."
Ecclesiastes 9:11

Often discipline requires us to act upon new information, or developments that we had not anticipated. Before we act to exploit new opportunities, we must discipline our mind to take the time to give it serious thought. What is before us could be a real breakthrough, or it could be a scam, or something that would just lead us down a rabbit hole that will waste our valuable time and money. In today's age of instant access to information, there is no excuse for failure to research any topic as much as required. Do not confuse discipline with the rush to just get something done. While it is true that procrastination is a terrible vice that must be removed from your life. Carefully analyzing any important action before taking it will save you from spending untold time and effort, which will not move you closer to your goal.

Remember the saying, "Work smarter, not harder." We must find the most efficient way to accomplish a task. Understand that the mind must be disciplined first, because self-discipline always begins with making a decision. The mind then commands the body, and the body acts to change the things around you which are under your control. Discipline always begins in the mind and it leads us to act in harmony with our goals and values. It is not mindless action in obedience to a command. We must know and agree with the rationale behind it, otherwise, it will not continue and it will have no power. God gave us minds to reason, to create, and to build. He gave us dominion over nature unlike any other creature. The power of intelligent thought will always outpace the use of mindless physical labor.

> *"Persistence and determination alone are omnipotent."*
> *Calvin Coolidge*

Perhaps persistence should be the subject of a chapter all on its own. But when you think of it, persistence is simply the continuous application of discipline toward a specific goal. And from a human standpoint, persistence and determination are omnipotent. It is because these principles can overcome lack of money, lack of resources, lack of connections, lack of consensus, lack of physical strength, or lack of any other advantage which might make success come easier to others. When we study highly successful people in any field, we find a long train of failures, obstacles, criticisms, and almost endless experimentation. It is only persistence powered by a strong vision, which can overcome all of these, given enough time.

> *"Now faith is being sure of what we hope for and certain of what we do not see."*
> *Hebrews 11:1*

Faith is linked unbreakably to discipline and persistence. It is the clear vision of what you do not yet see in the natural. Faith is the impetus which drives you to do the things that your mind and body rebel against in order to achieve the reward. That reward which exists only in your mind until it manifests itself in reality. This is not about just affirming what you want to happen, or trying to speak something into existence. You must take steady, affirmative actions in order to achieve your goal. And that goal must be possible, and within your power to accomplish it by yourself. If it is, you will know that it will be reachable with enough time and effort. God has promised his people certain things in his word that we can have faith and trust in because He has taken on the responsibility to perform them. But in other areas of life, God gives us the tools to influence the world around us, and to play a part in realizing the destiny He has designed for us.

With discipline powered by faith, you can build a great business, accumulate a fortune, greatly improve your health, strength, and physical appearance, or anything else that you have the vision to accomplish. Even small and painless acts of discipline can really surprise you over time with the liberating and life changing results. With every paycheck you receive or monthly business profit, you should set aside at least ten percent to put away in a savings account first, and then use the rest to live on. You must pay yourself first, because if you do not have the discipline to budget for all of your expenses, including giving and leisure, you will end up spending all of your income and not remember where it all went. It is the money that you set aside, beyond what you need for expenses, that is the seed for your future wealth.

The money that you have to spend to live, such as rent, mortgage, car payment, utilities, clothes, food, etc. is not really yours. You are enriching others who are supplying what you need and want. It is only the money that you set aside, not committed to these expenses, that is free to invest and grow into financial independence. This is why you should always live below your income as to maximize the amount that you can save and invest regularly. Remember, it is more important what you do with your money than how much you make. You must carefully plan your course of action to achieve any goal, but do not be too rigid in your approach. If you find that a certain plan is not working, slow down or stop, and then analyze why it is not working. Switch gears and make a change. It is not a violation of discipline or persistence to stop doing what does not work, if you start taking action that works, or works better. This is a perpetual process on your journey to success, which has no end.

Self-control and discipline must be developed within and kept with you as strong allies in your struggle. Yes, life is a struggle and filled with disappointments and pain. This is true for every human on earth, although people face different kinds of challenges. Everyone must pay their dues sooner or later. But everyone has the choice to conquer their circumstances, or be conquered by them.

CHAPTER 3

KNOWLEDGE

"The discerning heart seeks knowledge, but the mouth of a fool feeds on folly."

Proverbs 15:14

Knowledge becomes your pathway to survive and prosper in every aspect of life. In almost every profession, knowledge is needed to succeed, from a doctor, to a mechanic, to a farmer, to an engineer, to a chef, and everything in between. It is knowledge which allows you to provide for yourself and your family. Among most occupations, typically, it is the ones which require the most detailed and specific knowledge that pay the most, and yield the highest financial rewards. A few professions require years of formal, higher education along with the degrees required to certify completion. But with most other jobs, people either receive training from their employer or simply learn by doing from on the job experience. This is why when you get an entry level job, you should learn all that you can about the business you are working for, and be willing to take on more responsibilities as opportunities arise.

It should be understood that all forms of learning are equally valid, whether it is from books, formal training, or hands on experience. And in most cases, all may be required to one degree or another. The same is true for those who choose the entrepreneur path. But before you dive into the waters of operating your own business, you should already have a good working knowledge of how that business runs. This knowledge may be derived from working for someone else in that business, finding a friend or mentor in that business, or from getting independent education and training. But beware of so-called experts and gurus in some fields who make more money selling their courses than they do operating the business that you want to learn about.

In the world of internet and instructional websites of all kinds, information can be obtained either for free, or at very low cost. This is why it is a good idea, especially for young people, to intern or acquire an entry level position in a business or industry that they are interested in. Where in the past, many professions and industries kept their methods and practices as closely guarded secrets. But today, and more so in the future, these barriers are crashing down due to the explosion of information on any subject from a wide variety of sources. So find out everything you can about the business that you are in or want to be in. Make every effort to understand not only how things work, but why they work. Then you can problem solve, make improvements, and eventually be able to design systems which will move your business further than others. But in order to be able to take the time and effort to learn your business well, it should be in a field that you are passionate about and highly committed to.

When I was a teenager and a young man, all I wanted to do in my life was to make movies. I loved movies and I wanted to tell my own stories on film. Back in ancient times, when I was growing up, there were no smart phones, no internet, no video cameras for home use, (until a few years later) and no social media. Movies were filmed on rolls of plastic, photographic, film stock. And with very few exceptions, sound was not simultaneously recorded on film along with the visual images. I grew up in a lower end, working class household, where money was very tight. But on my twelfth birthday, my parents gave me their used, spring wound, 8mm movie camera as a gift. I thought then, and I still believe, that was the best birthday gift that I had ever received. Before that day, I would often use the camera to shoot scenes on family outings, etc. I practiced taking steady and well composed shots that were not the typical jerky, haphazard, camera work of most home movies. As time went on, I became more knowledgeable, which released my creativity and experimentation.

Eventually, I would make short films which told different stories, and use my friends from school as actors. I would build sets and models in our garage, and sometimes make or use costumes. Filmmaking became my obsession, and that is all I wanted to do as a career. Part-time jobs would pay for my efforts, as my films became better and more sophisticated with each one. I attempted to raise the production value of my films by upgrading equipment, buying dozens of books on all aspects of filmmaking, and incorporating special visual effects (not CGI) as the subject matter demanded. Although, I had no connections in the industry, I continued to make my self-financed, independent films. As a very young man, I married my wonderful wife, and worked different full-time jobs to maintain our household. I never did establish a viable career in the film industry; however, I did successfully create several films of which some have gone on to video distribution, television and film festivals. This personal account was to illustrate the power of persistence and self-taught knowledge.

"Test everything. Hold on to the good."
1 Thessalonians 5:21

Be careful, because not all of the information that you hear, see or read is relevant or accurate. Based on my experience with reading self-help books or enrolling in educational courses, I can break down all of the information into three general categories. **1.** False – Some of the teachings do not actually work. They are based on faulty premises or incorrect science, math, or psychology. And some of what is taught may be technically true or work in theory, but does not work in real world application. **2.** Outdated or irrelevant – Here, the information is or was accurate, but is no longer an effective system to use in your current market or industry. For example: My wife and I enrolled in an expensive real estate course offered by a very wealthy expert who had built up a large portfolio of properties using techniques which he had developed years prior, and in a totally different market situation. Often, specific techniques and formulas which worked for one person, at one time, will not automatically transfer over to you. **3.** True knowledge – This is information that you can actually use, and is relevant, and helpful. Most of this knowledge is based on true principles, rather than any specific technology or technique. If you learn how to apply enduring principles to your current situation, you will not just be stuck with expensive and outdated knowledge.

When you acquire knowledge or learn something new, ask yourself why this works. And what principles apply to this situation? Then, when technology, laws, culture, or markets change, you will be able to adjust your systems and techniques to the current climate, based on the same principles. Even though I give real world applications of principles, the principles are universal and eternal. I did not invent them or discover them. I discovered them for myself after many years of trial and error, and continuous searching. Every technology and invention that we now have, and all the knowledge that we have gained, is a result of the application of universal principles. These principles are self-evident and verifiable because they are truth. They are wisdom which will never diminish with changing times. And they are the basis of all knowledge.

CHAPTER 4
STRATEGY

The title of this chapter is strategy rather than strategies, because it is not a list of various strategies. It is to point out that you must have a strategy to succeed in any event where the outcome is uncertain. A strategy is simply a plan that you employ to achieve a specific objective. A good strategy can often win over superior strength, numbers, or advantage. It takes much intelligent thought and effort to invent a winning strategy. This principle has been used for thousands of years by military leaders, businesses, politicians, investors, gamblers, and coaches. The military teaches officers about historic strategies, and why they were successful or unsuccessful, even though the technology involved was long outdated.

In developing a winning strategy, it is important to fully understand your opponent. Your opponent could be anyone or anything that you want to win against, whether it is a rival football team or the stock market. If you don't have knowledge of what you are dealing with, and a plan on how to win, you will most likely lose. One way to develop a winning strategy is, after you have studied to understand your opponent, then you must take a realistic look at yourself. What are your strengths and what are your weaknesses? Try to lead with your strengths and then try to conceal your weak points, or at least don't depend on them to play anything but a minor role. Your strengths could consist of experience, specific knowledge that your opponent is unaware that you possess, hidden assets, misdirection, cunning, courage, and much more. But you should not in normal practice, try to harm or deceive anyone, because no lasting success comes from that. A strategy must be designed to fit the business or challenge that you are engaged in. Strategies may have to be altered or modified based on success or lack of it. Remember, keep doing what works, and or do it more. Stop doing what does not work, and or do it less. Start with safe and simple strategies at first, until you gain more confidence in your knowledge and skill. For example: When I was dabbling in different businesses or investments, quite often I found myself losing money. So I would cut back on pouring more money into something until I could figure out why it was underperforming. While I did my research, I would just start saving money, instead of continuing to lose it in any venture that was too risky, or one that I did not fully understand. I found that I could never lose by saving money. And I would have more ammunition to use for a legitimate opportunity when it presented itself.

It is important to minimize risk at all times, no matter how much you know or think you know. And you should be content with small profits coming in regularly over time. These are general strategies to build lasting wealth. As Solomon said,

"Dishonest money dwindles away, but he who gathers money little by little makes it grow."

Proverbs 13:11

When engaged in the same or similar activities over and over, it is useful to develop a fixed strategy or a best strategy for each activity. As I played and learned various casino games, I would place small bets on fixed bankrolls. After analyzing the probabilities for each bet, along with the volatility of the game itself, I would come up with the size of bets, the number of bets, and when to exit. Then I would write out on my computer and print out these "one sheets" as I called them. These would outline how to play and how to bet for the best results. Of course, these strategies did not guarantee a profit with every session. But they did help me to lose less and walk away with profits (even smaller ones) much more frequently than I would if I had no plan or strategy.

Even the best and most thought out

strategies will not be successful every time. So every good strategy must have alternatives if things don't go the way you expect them to. This means incorporating a plan **B,** or **C,** or **D,** depending on what your opponent does. In the game of chess, for example, What if you want to sacrifice a less valuable piece, hoping that your opponent would take it, and thus expose his queen to be taken by another one of your pieces? But instead of taking the bait, he makes a different move which places your own queen in direct danger. You must anticipate all of the different moves that your opponent may make against you. In short or intermediate term stock trading, you take on a position which makes logical sense based on the recent price movements of the stock. But if the trade goes against you beyond an acceptable limit, you need to exit the trade immediately or place a stop limit order that will automatically be triggered if the price falls to that level. Always plan an escape to cut or to minimize losses if things do not go your way. You must survive to fight another day.

Remember this very important fact. In almost every action we take or venture that we engage in, there are no certainties, but only probabilities. Our job is to do everything in a way that will give us the highest probability of success. And in time, as you win more than you lose, you will be successful. Finally, a successful strategy must be based on true and current knowledge or mathematically sound or scientifically proven principles. If you have tested the information or principles on which your strategy is based, then implement it over and over again. And do it with confidence and boldness.

When you apply your successful strategy to a one-time challenge, your probability of coming out ahead is greatly increased. If it is an on-going effort to master a particular discipline such as stock or option trading, real estate investing, or even casino gambling, keep going and practice the strategy until you master it. You will not win every time, but when it doesn't work out, analyze why it didn't, and make any minor adjustments to correct the problem in the future. But remember, when you develop or change a strategy, always make sure that you act on actual facts and true principles, and not just on people's opinion. There is an old saying in the field of stock market trading, "Act on what you see, not on what you think." So, do not let the occasional setback cause you to give up.

CHAPTER 5

MONEY MANAGEMENT

"Suppose one of you wants to build a tower. Will he not first sit down and estimate the cost to see if he has enough money to complete it? For if he lays the foundation and is not able to finish it, everyone who sees it will ridicule him, saying, 'This fellow began to build and was not able to finish'."

Luke 14:28-30

Note, that in the above passage, the Lord was making a comparison of the normal and expected practice of cost estimation and budgeting, to the cost of following Him. But it highlights the seriousness of following these steps with every activity of life where significant allocations of funds are involved.

On the macro level, it is wise to have a personal or family budget which accounts for all of your take-home income and how it is to be distributed among all of your expenses for each period, usually monthly. This is useful even if you can only estimate certain expenses or your income. It is important to order your life so that your expenses do not regularly exceed your income. If they do, you must quickly adjust to increase your income i.e. work more hours, get a second job, or a side business which requires only small investments, but produces fast returns. Of course, your other option is to reduce your expenses until they fall below your income level. In most cases, at first, you will have to do both. Budgets can be as different as people, each have different needs, challenges, goals, and income. But the important thing is to do whatever you need to, to make the math work.

In figuring out a budget, you should

always pay yourself first. This means that no less than ten percent of your monthly income should go into a savings account. This account will be used for unexpected emergencies only, not vacations, birthdays, or nights out. Nor should it be comingled with any money allocated for any other purpose. When this account equals your average monthly income, then start putting your savings into another account which you can call an **investment account.** You should continue to save money into this account without limit and without end. The money in this account should be used for a business, investing, or any money generating opportunity. Many people use an I.R.A. for this purpose. If you should need to use any part of your emergency fund, then replace that money first, before contributing to the investment account. When your emergency fund is back to its prior level, then continue to put money into your investment account.

While you are regularly growing your investment account, you should be studying the types of businesses or investments that you are interested in. The basic first rule for investing is that you want to get in at a discount. Don't try to get into the hottest thing at top dollar, or buy high priced shares of stock in companies that don't make any income or profits. Instead, you should look for bargains, buying things that are in demand, but the cost is well below its true value. Every successful business in the world, no matter what it is, acquires assets which could be products, services, labor, talent, etc. at a discounted price, then sells it to their customers at a higher price. Investing in assets that produces a regular income, or that increases in value and can be sold for a profit, is the time tested way in which many people build real wealth.

Budgeting money on the macro or big picture level for your family expenses, and investments, is a basic requirement for money management. But as you move further along your success journey, you may get into businesses or investments which require their own specific micro or limited budgets for each of those activities.

All businesses, no matter what size, must have their own operating budgets.

If you invest in stocks, ETF's, or mutual funds, you may want to dollar cost average into them. This means to invest the same amount of money every month, no matter what the price. So you are buying more shares when the price is lower and fewer shares when the price is higher. Or if you are trading securities on a shorter term, you build up a trading account, and then allocate a maximum fixed percentage for each trade. Consider risk management and probabilities in your money management plan. Beware of activities that demand high or unknown risks for the hope of achieving uncertain gains. One reason why I was so fascinated by certain gambling games is that the probabilities for each outcome are fixed and known, unlike a regular business or playing the stock market. For investments that most people consider traditional, any number of unknown variables could come into play and throw you off target, causing you to lose money. But in games such as roulette, baccarat, craps, or even blackjack, the probabilities for each outcome is set and unchangeable. Now, it is up to you to learn what they are, and how much risk you will assign to them. But if you treat gambling like a business, you will make smaller, lower risk bets, and then be satisfied with a small profit in each session, and have the self-control to leave.

The average recreational or even compulsive gambler might walk into a casino with $500. and not want to leave until he has turned it into $5000. But the smart or professional gambler might walk into a casino with $5000. and leave after he has made a $500. profit. The first would be highly improbable. But the second would be highly probable. Money management, if backed by self-control and discipline, has turned many a "no-win" situation into a success story. It is at the very heart of winning financial transactions. But let me point out one landmine that you may encounter before you realize it, and that is the emotion of greed. Greed can overtake you before you are aware of it and rob you of success and everything you have achieved.

So, that is why you must put into your money management plan or business plan, exactly how much you are willing to risk on an investment and how much profit on a percentage basis that you are willing to take. This must be fixed in your mind or recorded before you enter into any transaction.

Be content with profits that are probable under the circumstances. You should not try to hold out for sky-high profits that might be possible, but highly unlikely to occur. You should look only for the highest probabilities, not remote possibilities. This is why I think that very rigid strategies can and should be applied to casino games. However, in other areas such as business or investments, the probabilities of any outcome are not so fixed, but they often can be reasonably estimated. It is logical in the management of funds, to allocate a larger percentage of your investment funds to higher probability deals, and a much smaller part of your money to lower probability, higher risk deals. I think it is fine to put a few dollars into a slot machine, or buy a couple of lottery tickets once every month or two. But do not be consumed with these things, because they are just a shot in the dark. If you win something, then take the money and run. But never allow high risk bets to eat away at any of your significant time or money. Remember the three principle factors to consider before you commit funds for any item. **1.** NEED – Is the expense actually needed to survive, carry my business forward or to generate returns? **2.** RISK – Is the reward worth the risk? Are there better or safer ways to accomplish the same thing? Is this the best use of my money at this time? **3.** PROBABILITY – Remember that higher probability and safer investments can demand a larger portion of your investment capital. Whereas, when probability of success decreases, and risk is higher, the portion of your investment funds committed to such ventures must correspondently decrease. There is no real harm in taking a long shot once in a while with a very small amount of money. But even if you should win, don't become addicted to these types of bets.

Finally, as I stated before, increasing

your wealth is fundamentally a function of mathematics, and it is simple, elementary school mathematics. This is why so many average people, who never went to college or understood higher math, have built very successful businesses or have become successful investors. Your money management plan, whether it is in the form of a budget, spreadsheet, or profit and loss statement, is your 9th grade math workbook. It allows you to reconcile your expenses against your income to clearly show you whether or not you are being profitable.

CHAPTER 6
EXPERIMENTATION

"I have not failed. I've just found ten thousand ways that won't work."

Thomas Edison

Y ou don't have to be an inventor, scientist or high tech engineer to experiment. Many people in various walks of life have tried different things over and over, in an effort to develop a product or system that works better, is more efficient, or more profitable. In fact, ordinary people are where experimentation occurs the most. The days where a determined, lone inventor, working in his garage workshop or kitchen table on a world shaking breakthrough, is fading away fast. Today, most major innovations are developed in corporations with well-funded teams of specialists who can rely on current information available from anywhere in the world, with a few clicks of a mouse or keyboard. Of course, the end result of this kind of experimentation has often been legally protected and rewarded handsomely.

But the rest of us can freely experiment for our own purposes and benefit. We can all use the scientific method to test things and to draw conclusions based on the results. You don't have to have degrees on your wall or letters after your name to question, research, form a hypothesis, experiment, analyze data, and draw a conclusion. The vast secrets of nature do not care who discovers them or who finds new ways to put them to use. The fact is that technology and systems will constantly advance because knowledge builds on knowledge. This is true, not only for the big advances of the world, but for your own home, farm, or business. You can design, test and implement systems to improve efficiency and profit in your life.

So, whatever your business or interest in life may be, keep trying and testing new things.

Always try to adopt Edison's attitude toward things that did not work out as expected. Learn what does not work so you can eliminate those things, and you can move closer to discovering things that do work, and which could change your life. After you have gleaned all the available information you can on a subject, then customize that knowledge for your own use. For example, suppose you are interested in making internet videos and you are relatively new to the field. You know the type of content that you want to provide, and you have also researched cameras, lighting, editing software, and all of the technical necessities. But because of factors like your budget, space, location, etc., you can't afford the most advanced equipment, elaborate studio sets, exotic locations, etc. So you try out different techniques on a smaller scale, and make the most out of what you have. This is what drew me to film and video production years ago. It is a medium in which images can be totally manipulated and worlds can be created on the screen. So it doesn't matter what the sets are made of, or whether they have backs, sides, or a ceiling. Miniatures can be made to look full scale, and a distant location can be composited behind your subject by means of a green screen in your studio. The only thing that matters is that the image looks the way you are trying to create it on screen.

All of this to say that there can be many ways to achieve inexpensive yet effective results. Experiment with the resources you have and then test the results with your viewers or customers. In your experimentation of various processes, you may find that you will reach two kinds of conclusions, depending on what you are testing. The two types of conclusions that you may reach are, **1.** ABSOLUTE or **2.** RELATIVE. Absolute conclusions or solutions are more rare because they represent a major breakthrough in the answer that you are searching for. It is absolute because, if repeated the same way, under the same conditions, it will work every time. These are things like functional inventions, medical breakthroughs, and the discovery of a mathematical formula or a natural law. These things are not created, but discovered, and if properly applied to various problems, will produce consistent results. Relative conclusions are more commonly found, because these are processes that might work most of the time, but not all of the time. The main reasons for this are, **1.** The process may be good, but not perfect, and can never be made to be perfect or absolute. **2.** There are one or more variables which cannot be removed from the process.

In many formulas of math or science, there are elements known as "constants", and other elements known as "variables". Constants are things that are fixed, and do not change. Variables can be one or more elements or factors that can change in value, thereby affecting the outcome of the final results. And in most cases, we are only looking for systems and methods that work more reliably and consistently. Remember that in most things, we are looking for higher probabilities, not guarantees. It is also important that you allow enough time and resources to experiment properly. Do not be afraid to try and fail over and over, as long as you are moving closer to a successful result. When you do finally find the answer or system you are looking for, you will then own something that will be worth hundreds or thousands of times your investment. But this answer is something that you must ultimately discover for yourself. When you discover it, you will not only own it for life, but you will fully understand it and be able to modify or improve it as necessary.

Experimentation can be done on a small scale. Your only goal at first is to find a process that works most of the time. Note that any system based on mathematics or natural law, which works on a small scale, will work proportionately as well on a larger scale. So once you have discovered a winning system, you can gradually ramp it up for bigger results.

As any true scientist or researcher will attest, one of the most important things that you can do is to document every experiment thoroughly. Create a form or worksheet in which you can record every detail of each trial and the results thereof. Conduct several trials using the same factors, and then alter one of the factors to see how that affects the results, if at all. By carefully documenting each element of an experiment, you will begin to discover which methods work best and why. For example, in trading stocks and options for extra income, I began to experiment with different stocks, different option expiration dates, different strike prices, and different entry and exit targets. By documenting these variables and more for each trade, I discovered what percentage increase that I could set my profit targets at for the highest probabilities of making a modest profit most of the time. The end goal of experimentation and documentation is to develop a process that yields a profit most of the time.

Realistically, the profit per transaction may be small, such as several dollars per option contract. But as you are winning and your account grows, you can add more contracts or increase your investment little by little, using the same system with the same ratios. Without getting into probability graphs, and Markov chains, it is a mathematical certainty that the closer your end target is to your starting point, the higher the probability is that it will be reached. This is why you should set your target profit low enough to be easily reachable within the time frame or trials allotted to achieve it. When after experimentation, you find your winning process; just slowly increase your investment each time to make your profits grow.

CHAPTER 7

CYCLES, TRENDS, AND STREAKS

"There is a time for everything, and a season for every activity under heaven."

Ecclesiastes 3:1

M ost of us have identified cycles, trends and streaks in so many areas of life. We see them in everything from the stock market to casino games. They exist in business, shopping habits, and even political activities. The difference between these three phenomena is time and consistency. So, let us define these three things so we can identify them and understand how we may profit from recognizing them when they occur.

STREAKS – These are the shortest in duration. Streaks are the uninterrupted repeating of the same outcome in any given event. When the ball on a roulette wheel lands on a black number five times in a row, or ten times in a row, that is a streak until the ball lands on a red number or a green zero. At that point, the streak is broken. If a coin toss turns up seven heads in a row that would be a streak of heads. Streaks more often occur when there are predominantly only two outcomes, and each outcome has approximately a 50 percent chance of occurring. It is only in cases where the probabilities are fixed and known, and is near 50 percent, that streaks can be played with any effectiveness at all. Now, you might see random streaks of repeated outcomes in other games or events. But those streaks have almost no potential to persist. As for the formerly described streaks, they have a tendency to persist in the short-term.

Streaks can be seen very frequently in

any binary event where the odds are nearly even. We know that they occur, but we don't know all of the mathematical or scientific reasons as to why they occur. Still, streaks tend to dominate in the short-term. The binary outcomes of winning or losing can also streak, as long as the chance for each is close to 50 percent. Any ties that occur should be considered as only a pause, but not a break in the streak.

Streaks can be seen regularly in many casino games. Most knowledgeable gamblers will tell you to bet with the streak, and ride it until it ends. Learn to recognize the signs of a streak forming and developing. One immediate repeat of an outcome could be the beginning of a streak. If two repeats happen, (three in a row) then a streak has formed. Your action should be immediate and short-term. You should bet with the streak until it ends. Although streaks tend to persist, they can end at any time. So understand that riding a streak will always be a short-term play, because streaks will always end.

There are many other areas of life where

streaks can be identified. If you look at a candle chart of a stock or other security, you might notice a streak of green candles indicating an upward move in price, or a streak of red candles indicating a downward move in price. So, if you wanted to time an entry point in a momentum trade, follow the direction of the streak. Do this with the understanding that to follow a streak in the immediate short-term only gives you a slight advantage of being right. And it should be understood that a streak can reverse at any time. Remember that we can only act on probabilities and not certainties.

TRENDS – Are the predominate movement of anything that fluctuates over time. They do not necessarily move in one single direction without interruption. But the overall move can be seen in one direction over a period of time. Trends develop over much longer time frames than simple streaks. And because trends show their predominance over longer time frames, even against more variables, they are a much stronger and more reliable indication of future direction. There is an old saying in stock trading, and even in casino games, "the trend is your friend." And there is much truth in this statement. Even though trends are powerful and should be followed, they exist in various durations. If you were to look at charts which track different stocks or securities, you can find uptrends, downtrends, or trends moving sideways. These trends can last for a couple of weeks, to a few months, to a year or more. When you look back in time at a long chart record, you can visually see where a trend ended, reversed and moved in the other direction. So trends also have time frames in which they exist. Trends will at some point end or reverse, but there will usually be notable reasons and signs when this begins to happen. It is therefore necessary for you to identify the direction that your security or investment is moving.

Be aware that the longer the trend has been established, the stronger it is and the more reliably it can be used to predict future results. But you would not want to base a long-term investment on a short-term trend. You should look for investment horizons which generally match the length of the trend that you are tracking. Since we know that trends can reverse, look for signs that the trend is weakening or losing steam. In the stock market, we can see price action stalling and volume drying up. If a security has made a strong, rapid (parabolic) move upward to new highs, and then starts to stall, you will probably see a trend reversal to the downside. After you identify the trend that is currently in place, research the reasons why and determine for yourself, how sustainable they are. But never bet against a trend that is in place. Wait for it to clearly reverse, and then go with the new direction.

Many stock traders look for different signs of a possible trend reversal. These could include chart patterns such as double top, double bottom, head and shoulders pattern, moving average crossover, and many more. Identifying these chart patterns as well as other indicators is known as technical analysis. But the experienced trader, who sees these signs begin to form, will only see them as warning signs or opportunity signs that the current trend may reverse direction. The wise move would be to hold back and not make a move until it is clearly established that the current trend is going to either continue, or reverse and move in the other direction. Also, you should understand that there are always reasons for trends to form and/or reverse direction. These reasons are not completely known, but with the wide variety of variables that could affect such things, some reasons are stronger than others. So among the chaos of variables that affect trends, we should focus on those factors which carry the most weight. As stated before, following current strong trends, like most other principles, only gives us increased probabilities, never absolute certainties.

CYCLES – These are recurring strong movements or trends which return after periodic absence. As trends extend over a longer timeframe than streaks, cycles move over a longer timeframe than trends. A cycle is a major movement which appears, and is strong, but then gradually or suddenly fades out. It then reappears at some point again. There are basically two kinds of cycles, **1.** REGULAR OCCURRING CYCLES are mostly found in nature. These include cycles of the moon, stars and planets, the changing seasons of the earth, the mating cycles of different animals, etc. **2.** IRREGULAR OCCURRING CYCLES for our purposes, these are the ones that we will be more concerned with. These are cycles largely controlled by the activities of humans. Examples of these types of cycles would be economic cycles such as recession, depression, or inflation. Market cycles such as Bull markets or Bear markets are also clearly evident looking back in history. We can also see business or sector rotation that track which industries are doing well, and which are out of favor.

A card table that is paying out wins hand after hand, or the slot machine that keeps winning for you are other examples of cycles. These are all examples of human activities or devices that can drastically change major outcomes based on a number of factors. Irregular occurring cycles cannot always be predicted, but they can be recognized. When a targeted activity starts to dominate in one direction, and that direction can be advantageous to you, then you should act upon it when you see the cycle turn in your direction. For example, let's say that you owned a second home that you are now using as a rental property. You would like to sell it someday when you can get a good sale price, but the real estate market is down in your area, and sellers have cut their asking price way down to close a deal. So you wait a year or so, and demand for housing in your area starts to increase, and maybe the Fed lowers interest rates, so the market in your area has turned from a buyer's market, to a strong seller's market. Now, buyers are bidding above your asking price, trying to lock in a home before the price rises even further. You identify that the cycle has turned in your direction and you list your house for sale, capitalizing on the up cycle. By the way, this also works in reverse. If you were in the market to buy, you would wait for a downturn cycle or a buyer's market.

> *"Be fearful when others are greedy, and be greedy when others are fearful."*
>
> *Warren Buffett*

You will always know when a cycle has turned in your direction. But you will not always know when it peaks or when it will end. Normally, you have plenty of time to act. But don't get greedy. You will almost never sell at the highest price possible or buy at the lowest price possible, and if you do, it will be purely by accident.

Taking advantage of cycles is not looking for the hottest new thing; rather it is looking for reliable, old things to become hot again. Waiting for a cycle to come back around should not be a full-time job. You should be managing your investments with different time frames, all with the intention of maximizing profits by considering trends and cycles.

CHAPTER 8

RISK AND REWARD

In many activities of life, we calculate the risk / reward equation very subjectively. This means that people value things like time, work, or relationships differently. And people view rewards for their efforts differently also. Some value personal satisfaction, freedom, or leisure as to them, more valuable than money. But for the purpose of this chapter, we will consider this equation in a purely mathematical and financial way.

Risk to reward is often expressed as a ratio. If you were to risk $100. for the possibility of making $300. then we could say that the risk / reward ratio for that activity would be

1:3 or 1 to 3. But you cannot only consider what is possible to win, or your target goal. You must also consider the likelihood or probability of reaching your target given the amount of risk you are willing to take. In other words, your risk must be limited and fixed, but your reward can only be a probability, which may or may not be known. Still, we must all make a mental assessment of the value of what we are trying to achieve and the probability of reaching it, versus the risk that we must take for it.

In the area of stock trading or even casino gambling, we have either an account balance or a bankroll. These represent the total amount of money that we have dedicated for those purposes. But only a small amount of your account or bankroll should be risked for each trade or each session. If you notice after a while that you are losing more than you are winning as far as financial profit and loss is concerned, you should go back and reconsider your strategy and your risk. But it is possible to have strategies and risk management that are so strong that you can be wrong more than you are right, and still be profitable. This is a great place to be because the best of us can get the movement or direction wrong sometimes. But if you have discipline and systems which cut your losses short while acting only on the higher probability trades, mathematically it is still possible to be wrong more than you are right, and still be profitable. The probability of any event occurring is not dependent on how much money you have riding on it.

One major principle of acting on a risk / reward event is that the higher the probability of reaching your goal, the greater the risk you can take. Conversely, the lower the probability of reaching your goal, the lower the risk you should take. This is why you should not spend $1000. on lottery tickets every month even if you are financially well off. Instead, if you want, just spend a few dollars on them. You are still giving yourself a chance to win, but the low risk you are taking corresponds properly with the enormous odds against you. Another important fact to remember in the mathematics of probabilities is this: The closer your target is to the starting point, the higher the probability of reaching it. What this means is that it is easier and more probable to make a reasonable profit, than it is to shoot for an enormous or unwarranted profit. It is also wise to be aware of what is happening and time your entry into a high risk situation when the probabilities for success are the highest. For example, if you were a stock or options trader and looking at a chart to determine if a stock was about to make a strong move to the upside, you should look at several indicators that must all be in sync to suggest that the stock will move up strongly in the next few days or weeks. You should calculate the strength of the move by determining how close it is to hitting an area of resistance, if there is volume or momentum behind the move, and several other factors.

When multiple signals are in alignment, only then should you make your move to get in. Taking higher probability trades means that you can win more often and also trade more often. These types of trades are usually shorter in duration because your target will be closer to your entry point. You will not necessarily make a higher percentage profit per trade, but you will be able to make a larger number of profitable trades. Once you have established good entry and exit strategies, you can increase your overall profit by increasing the number of shares or contracts that you open the trade with. In short, when you consistently reach a certain profit level per transaction, then simply increase the number of transactions at the same profit level to make more profits in total. Even high probability risks should be mitigated if the trade should move against you enough to where you are not likely to recover. Unless you are a day trader with your eyes constantly glued to your computer screen while your position is still active, you must set an automatically triggered order called a stop limit order. This order will execute if your position falls below a certain level, to prevent potentially deeper losses. A stop limit is especially important for longer term trades that you cannot constantly monitor. If you cut short any large loss from every trade, then your actual risk per trade is always reduced.

But like insurance, a stop limit order should only be set to stop large or unacceptable losses. With the wide swings in the market, you could be stopped out repeatedly and unnecessarily if your stops are placed too close, giving you many small losses.

Once you are in a good profit position, then you can move your stops closer or use a trailing stop. This will help you lock in profits against any reversal. By taking high probability trades, and setting your target risk to reward at a modest 1 to 2, you can be wrong over 60 percent of the time, and still be profitable. This is because when you win, you will more than compensate for the small losses you will have. The key to maintaining a 1 to 2 ratio or higher is to allow enough time to let the trade hit its target. The problem is that too many traders cut their profits short and let their losses run. They just want to win anything and not be wrong. But the more times that you can double or triple your money, the fewer times that you have to be right. In other words, your larger wins will overtake and surpass your smaller losses.

The key to winning is mathematics, not emotion. Short term trading in stocks or options is in many ways like casino gambling. In both, you look at trends. In both, you limit your losses. And in both, when you win, you should take the profit and run. There are many situations in both trading and gambling when you might want to just take out a smaller profit, even if it is short of your target goal. This happens when your directional momentum seems to be running out of steam, or it starts to move against you and you want to lock in any profit that you already have. It is also interesting and fun to participate in games or activities which could offer a wide range of potential rewards.

So rather than targeting a fixed risk to reward ratio, you might want to watch and see what reward it may bring whether large or small. But as always, your total risk must be fixed and limited. An example of this would be to sit down at a slot machine and insert a twenty dollar bill. Your plan might be to cash out if you should double your money or more. If you stick to your plan, you limit your total risk, you have a reasonable probability of doubling your money, and you also have the possibility of hitting a major jackpot, all with the same twenty dollar risk. Again, if you hit your minimum target goal or higher, take your profit. Even a small profit is better than any loss. Think mathematically.

To sum it up, most of the time, risk to reward ratios cannot be known in advance, but only after the fact. This is because final outcomes are never guaranteed. You must know, or at least have a good idea of the probability of success. And it is upon that basis that you set your reward target. You should adopt sound strategies. You must set a reasonable risk amount and stick to it. Finally, if you are not winning more than you are losing, keep testing and making adjustments until you find the way to win.

CHAPTER 9

VOLATILITY

Volatility is the ability of anything to move, change, increase or decrease, and is usually characterized by the speed and amount that these can occur. In business or finance, we usually associate high volatility with high risk, and low volatility with low risk. So, anything that fluctuates over short periods of time can have its own inherent volatility rating. In the stock market, each stock is given a volatility score called the Beta. This number compares a particular stock to the average of the whole market. If a stock has a beta of 1.0 this means that the stock has the same volatility as the overall market, or the average of all stocks. A rating of less than 1.0 means that the stock is less volatile than the market average. A Beta higher than 1.0 indicates that the stock has a higher volatility than the market average. The volatility of the whole market can also change. There is an index called the VIX, which tracks the volatility of the whole market. In that type of setting, the emotions and actions of market participants raise or lower volatility. When the market panics or sells off with high volume, volatility usually goes higher. When people get back into the market and steadily start buying again, volatility will drop down.

There are even derivatives, indexes, and exchange traded funds (ETF) that people can buy and sell which trade only on market volatility. This type of trading can be extremely risky, because market sentiment can change at any time for any reason. Another common way to play different volatility levels is in casino games. Experienced gamblers know the volatility of different games and different bets. This would apply to everything from table games to slot machines. In all games of chance, volatility is considered high when the game could have very large payouts which occur rarely, and also fewer lower and intermediate payouts. In other words, if and when you hit a rare jackpot, you could win big, but most of the time, you will lose. Lower volatility games or bets offer lower payouts which come more frequently, but caps off the higher jackpots at a much lower level.

The key principle when it comes to volatility is that no matter how much or how little money you have, your investment in high volatility bets must be proportionately smaller, while bets in lower volatility events can be larger. There must always be an inverse correlation between volatility and money risked.

Volatility can be high or low in different businesses, professions, or jobs. Consider for example, a country store which sells seed, grain, and feed to farmers. They might also sell tools and farm equipment. The store may be located in a rural area, and may have been in business for the last 50 years, selling needed products to local farmers. In such a scenario, the proprietors may make a respectable, steady income, but they will never become excessively wealthy on that business alone. This would be a low volatility enterprise, because the risks are not very high, but neither is the reward. On the other end of the spectrum, you have a business innovator such as Elon Musk who invests many millions into new and far reaching technologies and products. Tesla Motors has reinvented the electric vehicle, making it fast, powerful, efficient and affordable. The factories that build the vehicles are new creations themselves. They have completely automated the assembly of vehicles with the latest computer and robotic technology. Without question, the investment of Musk and others was very high and very risky. But as of this writing, the investment has yielded super rewards, making Tesla one of the largest companies in the world, and Elon Musk one of the richest men in the world.

In higher volatility ventures, you should realistically assess your own knowledge, experience, talent, and skills. Most of the men who built the most successful businesses in the world, and did it from the ground up, did so after overcoming many challenges and taking extreme risks. They were driven and laser focused on accomplishing their objective. They also had a high degree of knowledge and insight into their field, even though what they produced was untested. So, just be realistic about your own abilities and the price you are willing to pay to get what you want. Remember, for every great success that the world celebrates, there are thousands who nobody ever hears about that never made it. Volatility and probability are also inversely correlated. That is to say, that the higher the probability any event will occur, the lower the volatility, and the lower the probability, the higher the volatility. Look at a roulette wheel for example. There are many different bets that can be placed with a wide range of volatility levels. If you bet on red or black, odd or even, or high or low, these have the highest probability of hitting. But they will only pay 1 to 1 or even money when you win. On the other hand, you can place your chip on a single number to win. This bet has the lowest probability of winning, but if it does, you will receive a nice 35 to 1 payout for your efforts.

Generally speaking, unless you are very wealthy or addicted to taking high risks, you should always calibrate your risk down when volatility is high. And you should feel freer to increase your risk as volatility becomes lower.

CHAPTER 10

RANDOMNESS OR DETERMINISM

"The lot is cast into the lap, but its every decision is from the Lord."

Proverbs 16:33

There still exists some controversy among scientists and mathematicians over the nature of randomness, or even if the concept truly exist. We usually define randomness as a decision or outcome which is not based on any definite pattern or predetermined cause. A random event would therefore be completely unpredictable by its nature. But if the probability of any event is fixed and known, the frequency of outcomes over many trials can be predictable. This does not mean that any one single trial or event can ever be predictable. Over many trials, the outcomes will come closer to matching up with their statistical probabilities.

So, what is randomness, really? Is it some unknown, mystical force that can never be understood? Or is there any such thing as true randomness? As laymen, we tend to describe any event which is unforeseen, unexplained, or unpredictable, as random. But is it really? Just because we do not know or understand the cause of something, does not mean that it had no cause. Maybe we can start to figure it out by looking at what a great English scientist discovered almost 350 years ago.

> *For every action, there is an*
> *equal and opposite reaction.*
> *Newton's Third Law*

This clearly implies that if we see a reaction, something of equal force had to produce it. Every motion and every effect has to have a cause, and that cause has to have the power to produce the effect. Yet so often, people think of randomness as an unknown, mystical force. Or even worse, that it can produce a desired result without the use of creative intelligence. One of the biggest and most pervasive examples of what I am referencing is the belief held by many scientists and by many people concerning the creation and advancement of biological life forms, including humans. Many believe and teach the unscientific and illogical notion that given enough time, and the right conditions, that inorganic material can become organic material, and that simpler life forms can advance themselves into more complex life forms. This idea is fundamentally flawed because nothing ever engineers itself into existence, or advances itself into more complex forms. Most people, who hold these beliefs, do so because they do not want to admit that an intelligent power is necessary to do any of it. They point out that given enough time and enough randomly occurring circumstances, eventually, the right combination will accidentally take place for it to happen. This idea defies all logic and known science.

Something that is impossible to happen, will never happen, however many millions or billions of years you give it. This thinking is similar to the mindset of the compulsive gambler or the chronic lottery player. The belief is in the possibility of winning without the concern for the overwhelming probability against it. The futile quest to understand the nature of randomness has caused many to stumble in the darkness of ignorance for centuries. It is only when men like Isaac Newton and others, started to try to understand why things work the way they do, and the causes behind them, that true science and rational thought began to flourish.

The belief that every event has a cause, whether we know it or understand it or not, is known as determinism. This gives us the basis for investigation and experimentation to discover causes and to gain more understanding of events that were typically thought of as just random. When we approach a problem with a deterministic mindset, we are then forced to look for the causes instead of just relegating it to chance. Some thoughtful people have searched for causes and have found at least some answers. Let us take the game of roulette for example. Back in the 1990's a Spanish gentleman named Gonzalo Garcia Pelayo, while playing roulette in his local casino, noticed that some numbers would hit much more often than others. He then decided to track and record the outcomes of thousands of spins, using the help of his family. Pelayo was not a professional scientist or mathematician, but he was able to identify the most frequently hit numbers on each wheel. What he discovered was ***wheel bias.*** This is any imperfection in the balance, manufacture, or mechanics of the wheel, which would tend to disrupt the even distribution of winning numbers. Since roulette wheels are designed and manufactured to create the most even distribution of winning numbers as possible, the presents of a pronounced imperfection or bias in the wheel, can make certain numbers or sections of the wheel, hit more often than probability dictates. The Pelayo family was certainly not the first or the last to exploit and profit from bias wheels.

Another effort to pierce the mystery of this random game was attempted back in the 1970's by two university physics students, Doyne Farmer and Norman Packard. These two brilliant students reasoned that the resting place of the roulette ball could be largely predicted based on taking measurements of the position of the wheel when the ball is released, the speed of the wheel, and the speed of the ball. They were so convinced of their hypothesis, that they developed hidden computers that they wore inside their clothing. These computers would record data that the students entered from tapping contacts inside their shoes, each time the ball passed a fixed point on the wheel. The computer then instantly analyzed and made a mathematical prediction on the section of the wheel that the ball was likely to land.

Their experiment, as crude as it was, proved that the laws of physics and nature can be understood and applied to anything in the physical world. The students did ultimately profit from the experiment, and both went on to make greater achievements in science.

In electronic games such as slot machines, video poker, and video keno, people have tried to duplicate the natural effects of randomness through artificial means. In each of these types of games, there is a micro processing chip called a **Random Number Generator.** This chip is programmed to cycle through thousands of numbers in fractions of a second. Each number corresponds with a final outcome on each spin when the start button is pushed. Most of the numbers are no-winners for the player. Some of the numbers correspond to small wins. A smaller set of numbers represent intermediate level wins. And a very small set of numbers will trigger a major win or jackpot if they happen to come up. These are determined by the settings desired by the casino, as well as the legal regulations that govern the operation of casino games in each jurisdiction. The random number generator continuously cycles these numbers around at thousands per second. When the player hits the start button, the winning or losing number is chosen, and the screen or the reels then display the result. This electronic method is effectively, no different than picking a ticket out of a spinning drum. It is no different than keno balls blown around by air in the clear plastic chamber, or any other randomization method to make the next outcome uncertain and unpredictable.

This example of artificial randomness is to suggest that even in man's attempt to copy the randomness of the natural world; we see that there must be a cause for every outcome. A human intelligence must create a computer program to reach certain outcomes at certain intervals. This is not random. This is deterministic. In fact, several years ago, a computer programmer who worked for the Nevada Gaming Control Board, of all things, was able to break the code of these programs enough to win jackpots on slot machines and video keno games. He was eventually discovered and spent some time in prison. But this is to demonstrate that man, with all of his intelligence and computers cannot create true randomness.

So in conclusion, my belief, based on strong evidence, is that nothing is truly random. Everything that happens is determined by a cause or several causes, whether or not we fully understand them. But this forms the basis upon which we can ask questions and seek the answers. Understand that we will never know every cause for every outcome in this world. But the more causes and forces that we can discover and understand, the greater control that we can have of predicting the probable outcomes of chaotic events. The principles of winning, all direct us to become better, never perfect.